The Brook Hill School

Writing Guide

M. Kent Travis

M. Kent Travis, *Brook Hill School Writing Guide.*

ISBN-13: 978-1475225761
ISBN-10: 1475225768

A Few Opening Thoughts on Writing

Ernest Hemingway, when asked what was the most frightening thing he ever encountered, answered: "A blank sheet of paper."

`When asked, "How do you write ?" I invariably answer, "One word at a time.'
~Stephen King

Writing is easy: All you do is sit staring at a blank sheet of paper until drops of blood form on your forehead.
~Gene Fowler

Write your first draft with your heart. Re-write with your head.
~From the movie *Finding Forrester*

The time to begin writing an article is when you have finished it to your satisfaction. By that time you begin to clearly and logically perceive what it is you really want to say.
~Mark Twain

"I am returning this otherwise good typing paper to you because someone has printed gibberish all over it and put your name at the top."
~English Professor (Name Unknown),
Ohio University

I'm not a very good writer, but I'm an excellent rewriter.
~James Michener

Contents

Introduction

The difficulty is not to write, but to write what you mean.
~R. L. Stevenson

To be honest, reading a writing guide is just not much fun. However, it is a necessary step in your advancement as a communicator with written words.

Here in these few pages you will find instructions for formatting papers as well as the basics of constructing *critical* essays according to MLA guidelines.[1] Think of these "instructions" as tools to help you gain a handle on the vocabulary of critical writing (at least the vocabulary we use here at Brook Hill). You will also find suggestions and examples of how to execute or put into practice what is required of you when you compose a critical paper. Again, this booklet is a *basic introduction.* You won't find the specifics of constructing and organizing arguments and proofs. Hopefully, you'll learn that as you progress from grade six to your senior year.

Writing a sound critical essay takes practice and thought, both of which are not that comfortable to us. However, once you master the basic elements of the critical essay you will be able to interact more effectively with your classmates and your teachers. In fact, many of our students have made us teachers re-think our understanding of things... many of us have been sharpened, taught, brought deeper in our thinking through your essays. And this, really, is one of the highest goals and delights of being in an educational setting, for both teacher and student.

We want to encourage you in your writing so that you can achieve a skilled written voice—a skilled soul-leading voice. Our desire is for us to engage in dialogue with each other and to expand our dialogue to include some of western civilization's greatest voices. This will, in turn, equip you in the dialogue of life and living, which will sometimes require the ability to write. Being able to write *well* will give you a stronger voice in the dialogue. This is why we teach as we do at Brook Hill and this is why this guide is here.

I must make an admission and give credit where credit is due. The terminology and general paragraph construction presented here comes from Jane C. Schaffer's work in the field of writing instruction. Also, much of my own thinking on writing has been shaped by Dr. Scott Crider from the University of Dallas. His class and his book, *The Office of Assertion*, have both been vast resources in very digestible sizes. To him I give thanks and much appreciation.

Soli Deo Gloria.
Kent Travis, Founder's Hall 2012

---

[1] That is, the guidelines of the Modern Language Association. There are numerous other formats for documenting research and critical writing, but at Brook Hill we follow MLA guidelines because they are widely followed in English and history departments at most universities.

General Pointers for Essay Writing

- Underline or *italicize* titles of books, major poems, and plays.
- Avoid contractions. They aren't appropriate in formal writing.
- If your sentence ends with a quote, place the period or comma inside the quotation marks, like "blah, blah, blah."
- Not all books are called a "novel." Make sure you call a book "book," an
  epic "poem" or "epic," a play "play," etc.
- ***Never*** let a quote stand by itself in a sentence. Embed your quotes. As most teachers would say, "Most of the time, not embedding your quotes is incorrect."
- When commenting on literature, use the **present** tense. Shakespeare may be dead, but he still speaks. (Just like you can still hear Beethoven, but he can't hear you.)
- When commenting on history, use **past** tense. The people, events, time periods, etc., that you are referring to already happened.
- "Proofread carefully to see if you any words out." ~Author Unknown
- If the simple, short word communicates what you want to say, use it. "One of the really bad things you can do to your writing is to dress up the vocabulary, looking for long words because you're maybe a little bit ashamed of your short ones." ~Stephen King
- If you don't *know* something, don't write about it as if you do.

Writing Terminology

These are the terms (from the Schaffer method) you will be using to identify the various parts of your critical essays at The Brook Hill School. Use this list as a quick reference for writing terminology.

THESIS (plural "theses"): the distilled or condensed argument of your essay. We will be using two kinds of theses:

> **MAJOR THESIS** (called **MT** for short)—in a full essay, this comes somewhere in your introductory paragraph, most often at the end. This sentence *identifies the major idea* that you will be discussing and *guides* the entire essay.
>
> **BODY THESIS** (called a **BT** for short; often called a TOPIC SENTENCE)—Each paragraph in the body of a paper begins with a BT. Each BT is a "proof" for your MT; it contains one of the reasons why you suggested the idea or opinion of your MT. A BT *guides* a body paragraph in the same way that the MT guides the entire essay.

CONCRETE DETAIL (called a **CD** for short)—specific details proving or supporting the BT. In literature or history essays, a **CD** means an example or quotation from the story or history book.

COMMENTARY (called a **COMM** for short)—commentary sentences give an opinion, interpretation, personal response, analysis, explication, insight, reflection, and/or speculation about or springing from the CD and always moving toward proving or explaining the Major Thesis.

CLOSURE (called a **CL** for short)—the final sentence in a body paragraph. *It does not repeat* the BT. It often sums up the spirit of your paragraph in a sentence. In a sense, it is more commentary and perhaps a transition as you work your way into the next paragraph and on to the conclusion of the essay.

CONCLUSION (called **CONCL** for short): the last paragraph of an essay. At this point in the essay, your thesis should be thoroughly proven or explained. This paragraph helps tie all the major ideas of the essay together.

a. sum up your ideas
b. reflect on what you said in your essay
c. give more commentary about your subject
d. make predictions based on what you've said in your paper

The conclusion paragraph gives the essay a "finished" feeling. It should not simply repeat what was said in the introduction or in the rest of the essay.

Quotes and Notes

Quotes and Notes is a method of getting key passages, along with your responses to them, down on paper before you organize your essay into paragraphs. Simply set up your paper with two columns. The left column will be for quotes (from literature, the history book, critical essays, etc.). The right column will be for any notes or observations you want to make about the text (see COMMENTARY definition on p. 7). These "notes" will likely become the meat for your COMMENTARY sentences. Write your tentative topic on the top line. Your notes page might look like the following:

Topic:

QUOTES:	NOTES:

Structure of a Body Paragraph

Introduction and conclusion paragraphs vary in length (at ***least*** 3 sentences). Body paragraphs can be any number of sentences, depending on the assigned structure. Various paragraph structures are outlined below.

A. The FIVE sentence paragraph:

Sentence 1: **BT**
Sentence 2: **CD #1**
Sentence 3: **Comm**
Sentence 4: **Comm**
Sentence 5 **: CL**

B. The EIGHT sentence paragraph:

Sentence 1: **BT**
Sentence 2: **CD #1**
Sentence 3: **Comm**
Sentence 4: **Comm**
Sentence 5: **CD #2**
Sentence 6: **Comm**
Sentence 7: **Comm**
Sentence 8: **CL**

C. The TEN sentence paragraph:

Sentence 1: **BT**
Sentence 2: **CD #1**
Sentence 3: **Comm**
Sentence 4: **Comm**
Sentence 5: **Comm**
Sentence 6: **CD #2**
Sentence 7: **Comm**
Sentence 8: **Comm**
Sentence 9 : **Comm**
Sentence 10: **CL**

D. The ELEVEN sentence paragraph:

Sentence 1: **BT**
Sentence 2: **CD #1**
Sentence 3: **Comm**
Sentence 4: **Comm**
Sentence 5 : **CD #2**
Sentence 6 : **Comm**
Sentence 7 : **Comm**
Sentence 8 : **CD #3**
Sentence 9: **Comm**
Sentence 10: **Comm**
Sentence 11: **CL**

Things to note:
A sentence unit composed of a concrete detail (CD) and at least two commentary sentences (COMM) is called a **CHUNK**. You may add more commentary sentences per chunk if your teacher requires it or you need it to explain your point.

This method of writing (called "chunking") is meant to be a tool, one that guides and informs the writer in the process of communicating ideas. With practice, writers will be able to actively interact with concrete information (CD's) and form sound, insightful analyses, opinions, interpretations, personal responses, explications, etc. (i.e., COMM's), as he or she seeks to develop an argument or explanation in writing.

Obviously, this method for constructing paragraphs is rigid. It is NOT the expectation that you always write paragraphs using multiple chunks per paragraph. A more advanced analytical paper (which is what you'll be doing by your junior and senior years) would be composed of paragraphs that resemble the following form:

Sentences 1-3: An explanation and lead-in to quoted material.
Sentence 4 (or so): CD
Sentences 5-9 (or more): Commentary
Closing Sentence

Incidentally, this structure fits with a good formula for doing written analyses. First, state your point. Second, quote a passage that supports your point. Third, explain how your point and the text relate and then explore this connection. (For a more detailed explanation of this, see Crider's *The Office of Assertion*, p. 35).

So then, after the "chunking" method has been mastered and you are comfortable with performing the art of crafting an argument or an explanation using quotes and commentary, you may use these elements as you see fit. Remember, the goal is not to simply master the "form." Rather, the form is to aid you in reaching the true goal, which is to become a clear, insightful communicator of ideas via writing.

Introductions

Now that we've discussed the general structure of an essay, let's talk about how to craft the various parts. There are basically two types of introductions used in research writing: the introduction to the essay or paper and the introduction sentence to each paragraph.

Introduction Paragraphs

The introduction to an essay or paper is usually a full paragraph. (For simplicity, we'll say that a paragraph is *at least* three sentences long.) This paragraph is crucial to the paper for it introduces the reader to your chosen topic. A good introduction will inform the reader of WHAT he or she will be reading about. This should be stated succinctly in the MAJOR THESIS (which is usually the last sentence of the paragraph). Likewise, the introduction should persuade the reader that the essay is even worth reading. In an introduction, you might name or describe important events, define key terms, and ask crucial questions. It is also helpful (though not always necessary) to allude to or even state plainly the major points to be covered in the essay.

As you may have figured out, introduction paragraphs contain more than just the MAJOR THESIS. They *introduce* in a way that is similar to a handshake or a greeting when you first meet a person. The writer's job is to break the silence for the reader—on common ground if possible. As the silence is broken, the writer seeks to present his or her case. This may be done abruptly or subtly, depending on your audience or purpose. The approach generally used is to start broad and then work toward the narrower MAJOR THESIS. This allows you to inform the reader of the general context of your topic before you dive into the specifics of your argument. Laying down a heavy MAJOR THESIS right away can be a turn-off or too abrupt or confusing. On the other hand, this may be your desired effect. Remember: the main purpose is to prepare your reader for what you will say by leading them smoothly to your MAJOR THESIS.

Below is a sample introduction paragraph:

Fairy tales and nursery rhymes are the stuff of childhood whimsy. Who can forget the happily ever after of Snow White or Sleeping Beauty brought about by a handsome prince and true love's first kiss? Humpty Dumpty and his great wall fall continue to bring the king's horses and the king's men to the rescue. The happy endings and the sing-song delight of nursery rhyme words can shape so much of a child's imagination. However, some of these so-called rhymes can be detrimental to a child's psyche and his moral development. After all, the "rock-a-bye baby" falls out of the tree and the old woman who lived in a shoe whipped (WHIPPED!) her kids soundly before putting them to bed! Though these two examples—of many—have surely had their negative effects on the youth of countless generations, the most detrimental of all the nursery rhymes is the beloved "Mary Had a Little Lamb." "Mary Had a Little Lamb" teaches children co-dependence, out-right rebellion, and to associate with the wicked.

Things to note:

- This paragraph begins broad and on common or familiar ground with the reader; most people are familiar with this subject. By giving a few examples from fairy tales and nursery rhymes the writer seeks to evoke emotions in the reader and to draw him into the discussion.
- The paragraph moves past common ground and puts a sort of shock on the reader: some of these stories and rhymes are *not* good for children. This acts as an attention getter because it is contrary to what the reader is expecting. Most likely, the reader will want to continue reading: "This idea is crazy," he or she might be thinking. "I need to see where this is going."
- Two "negative" examples are given to show that this idea is not so crazy after all.
- Finally, the writer comes to the text that he wants to focus on: "Mary Had a Little Lamb."
- He concludes with his MT and informs the reader that he will be focusing on three major problems with "Mary Had a Little Lamb": co-dependence, rebellion, and associating with the wicked.

→ Remember, this is the most common method of leading a reader into a MAJOR THESIS; it is not the only method. The key is to remember that when you are writing, there is certainly going to be a reader. Keep him or her in mind as you write and lead them along in a way that will have the most impact and effectiveness.

Introduction Sentences (Body Theses)

The BODY THESIS (or Topic Sentence) is the first sentence of a body paragraph. This sentence determines and directs the content of the body paragraph. It is important that the BT links smoothly with the preceding paragraph. This is often done with a transition word or phrase (like *first*, *second*, *third*, *as a result*, *in addition*, *however*, *above all*, *therefore*, *thus*, *then*, *in sum*, etc.). Remember, a body paragraph is part of a bigger whole; it must fit within that whole.

Below is a sample BODY THESIS that might follow the introduction paragraph above (p. 13).

To begin with, “Mary Had a Little Lamb” is detrimental to a child’s psyche because the rhyme embraces the concept of co-dependence.

Things to note:

- This BT “flows” from the introduction paragraph. It uses the transitional phrase: “to begin with.”
- Then, it gives an opinion or observation (the rhyme is “detrimental to a child’s psyche”) and it explains why the opinion or observation was made (“the rhyme embraces the concept of co-dependence”).

Concrete Details--Parenthetical Documentation

When writing a critical essay you will nearly always use quotes. This must be done in a clear manner that will avoid plagiarism. Plagiarism is stealing someone else's intellectual ideas or the way he or she expressed those ideas and then acting like they are your own. You know the adage, "Give credit where credit is due." However, this can clutter up an essay if done poorly. So what are we to do? The simple answer is, keep it simple. Follow these general guidelines:

1. **Quote accurately**. As far as the details of quoting go, see below and the following few pages for several examples. For now, remember to get quotes written down accurately. Leaving out a word or putting punctuation in the wrong place can be confusing and even weaken the point you're trying to make.
2. **Give the author's name and the page number.** The most common way to do this in an essay is to state the author's name as you give the context for your quote. Here is an example:

   In arguing for the proper approach to the Scriptures, Steve Schlissel states "God has not given us His oracles so we can cast a totem; He has given us His Word to recast *us* into the image of His Son" (250).

   - Note that the author's name is given in the sentence and ONLY the page number is given in the parenthesis at the end of the sentence.
   - Note also the punctuation: capital letters, a semi-colon, a period, an italicized word. This is exactly as the text appears in the original source. If you change anything, you need to note it in your parentheses.

   If it is too awkward to give the author's name in your sentence or if you want variety you can give his or her LAST NAME in the parentheses at the end of the quote:

   Christians must realize that "God has not given us His oracles so we can cast a totem; He has given us His Word to recast *us* into the image of His Son" (Schlissel 250).

3. **Record the cited source.** The final page of your essay will be a Works Cited page (see p. 23). Only author's names and page numbers are given in the essay. The rest of the source information is put in the works cited page, so be sure you record it accurately. The purpose of doing all this is to give credit where credit is due and to provide readers with what they need if they want to look up your sources and read more about your subject. The entry for the above quote is found on the sample works cited page in this booklet (p. 34).

Concrete Details--Embedding Quotes

Although a CONCRETE DETAIL could simply be a fact from history or a piece of literature, CD's are usually constructed by EMBEDDING a quote *into* a sentence of your own. "Embedding" is a somewhat difficult concept to grasp *if* you don't understand what the word means in the context of writing. Think of it in terms of gardening: you have soil in which you plant seeds. The part of the sentence constructed from your own words is like the soil. A quote is like the seeds that you plant into the words that are your own. You are, essentially, *inserting* the quote into your sentence to form a complete CD statement. By using this EMBEDDING technique of citing outside sources, you will be able to give the context of quotes as well as begin commentary on your BODY THESIS.

There are many ways to embed quotes. What follows are four samples of CD sentences using four different methods. These CD's were constructed based on the following passage from *A Short History of Western Civilization*:

> During a period of wandering in the desert of the Sinai Peninsula that followed the Exodus, there occurred a religious experience that gave fundamental shape to the religious consciousness of the Hebrews. Under the leadership of Moses, the Hebrews of the Exodus came to believe that they as a people had become special partners of Yahweh, whom at least some had worshiped during the age of the patriarchs. Master of history and of nature, as he had demonstrated through the events of the Exodus, Yahweh made a *covenant*, or mutual contract, with Moses' people: he selected them as his people and promised to care for them. (27)

- Note that this is an extended quote (more than 4 lines of the page). Extended quotes begin on a new line, are indented one inch from the rest of the text, and *do not* have quotation marks.
- Note that the citation is *outside* the period.

<u>Fragment—quoting a few words:</u>
Sullivan notes that under Moses, their new leader and guide, the Hebrews became convinced that they were "special partners of Yahweh," the God whom their forefathers had served (27).

<u>2 Fragments—splitting a quote with your own words :</u>
Moses was the great leader/guide who convinced the Hebrews that they "had become special partners of Yahweh," the God whom their "patriarchs" had served (Sullivan 27).

<u>**Paraphrase—stating the facts in your own words:**</u>

According to Sullivan, under the guiding power of Moses, the Hebrews eventually believed that they were a chosen people of Yahweh, the God worshiped by their forefathers (27).

<u>**Full Sentence—quoting a full sentence or passage:**</u>

Sullivan says the following about the Hebrews during the Exodus period: "Under the leadership of Moses, the Hebrews of the Exodus came to believe that they as a people had become *special partners* of Yahweh, whom at least some had worshiped during the age of the Patriarchs" (27, emphasis added).

Things to note:

- *Context* is set up prior to or after the quote is given. This gives the reader at least some idea of what you're talking about and where the quote comes from. This is difficult for many students. They either want to retell everything or they don't tell anything. Try to find a balance. You want the reader to "be on the same page" with you—to know what you're talking about. On the other hand, you *don't* want them to be bored with an artless or irrelevant retelling of a scene from a book. So then, retell enough to lead the reader along with you, but not so much that they're sleeping along the way.
- Only quote the most important parts of the sentence—paraphrase the rest.
- You usually name the source of the quote in the sentence.
- Only the page number itself is in the citation, unless the source is not named in the sentence or if you have changed something in the author's original text..
- ALSO, note that the parentheses COME AFTER the end quotation mark but BEFORE the end period.

Concrete Details--Special Cases

Quoting Scripture:

Scripture is alive and active, sharper than any two-edged sword (Hebrews 4:12). So we say that *it* speaks. However, some unknown "it" doesn't say anything in the Bible. Either the Bible speaks or a person (or being) *in* the Bible speaks

Wrong:

It says in the Bible, "There is no other name under heaven given to men by which we must be saved" (Acts 4:12).

In the Bible, it says, "There is no other name under heaven given to men by which we must be saved" (Acts 4:12).

Right:

The Bible says, "There is no other name under heaven given to men by which we must be saved" (Acts 4:12).

The Bible says that "there is no other name under heaven given to men by which we must be saved" (Acts 4:12).

Peter says, "There is no other name under heaven given to men by which we must be saved" (Acts 4:12).

The Bible asks, "And how can they hear without someone preaching to them?" (Rom. 10:14).

More Examples:

Okay: The Bible says, "Go into all the world and preach the good news to all creation" (Mark 16:15).

Good: Jesus said, "Go into all the world and preach the good news to all creation" (Mark 16:15).

Better: Jesus commanded his disciples, "Go into all the world and preach the good news to all creation" (Mark 16:15).

Best: Jesus instructed his disciples to "go into all the world and preach the good news to all creation" (Mark 16:15).

Changing a quote to make it grammatically correct

Much of Scripture (and other literature) is written in past tense. But, when writing about literature we use present tense, because we are discussing a living piece of literature. Therefore, it is sometimes necessary to change the tense of a quote to present tense in order to avoid interrupting the flow of the paper or essay. For example, if we quote Exodus 1:8 as it appears in the Bible it looks like this:

> The fate of the Israelites changed when "a new king, who did not know about Joseph, came to power in Egypt" (Ex. 1:8).

If we were writing about the Israelites from a historical perspective or with a historical focus, we would keep the tense as it is. However, if we are writing about the text as literature and not just reporting history, we need to change to present tense. This is done by changing the verbs to present tense and distinguishing the changes made to the quote with brackets. The brackets inform the reader that you are altering the quote. The changed CD would read as follows:

> The fate of the Israelites changes when "a new king, who [does] not know about Joseph, [comes] to power in Egypt" (Ex. 1:8).

Middle of quote eliminated:

Often times you won't need to use an entire quote, only key portions of it. To communicate to the reader that you have omitted some of the original sentence(s), use ellipsis points (that is, three periods—and ONLY three periods—in a row). For example, if we only want to quote a portion of Exodus 13:21 it might look like the following:

> The Lord showed his care for the Israelites in the wilderness, for by day He went "ahead of them in a pillar of cloud… and by night in a pillar of fire" (Ex. 13:21).

➔ You DO NOT need to use ellipsis points at the beginning or end of a quote:

Wrong:

Augustine once said, "…command what you wish, but give what you command."

Right:

Augustine once said, "command what you wish, but give what you command."

Commentary Sentences

For many students, grasping the conept of writing commentary sentences is difficult. However, if you remember that what you are doing in a critical essay is trying to prove or support a point (the MAJOR THESIS), the cloud that commentaries can be disperses. Commentary sentences are your *interaction* with ideas and quotes as you work to *prove* or *support* your point. They are the sentences that explain and hammer home the development of your ideas. Thus, these sentences are crucial, for they carry much weight in the overall scheme of the paper.

Commentaries show the link between your MT and your CD's. CD's aren't just "good" quotes that you've slapped down; they are quotes that contain the seed that supports or proves your argument. Without good commentaries, your MT is left unexplained or unproven and your CD's are next to worthless. So work hard to develop good commentaries, fleshing out the ideas contained in the CD's and always moving toward explaining or proving your MT. Remember that commentaries come in various forms: opinion, analysis, insight, interpretation, personal response, explication, reflection, and/or speculation.

Here are examples of commentary sentences that might follow the following BT and CD:

To begin with, "Mary Had a Little Lamb" is detrimental to a child's psyche because it embraces the concept of co-dependence. The first stanza of the rhyme states that "everywhere that Mary went,/The lamb was sure to go" (*Walt Disney's Mother Goose* 6).

Opinion: The thought that a lamb would follow a child around is absolutely absurd.

Analysis: However, if a lamb were to follow a child around, as Mary's did, then it must have been a particularly needy lamb, for it was "*sure* to go" wherever Mary went.

Insight: A particularly needy creature, human or otherwise, has a tendency toward abnormal behavior.

Interp: In the case of Mary's lamb, this abnormal behavior appears to be a form of co-dependence, as if the lamb cannot bear to be left alone. Also, as far as the reader knows, Mary does nothing to stop the lamb from following her "everywhere."

Response: This particular form of co-dependence is even more disturbing because it is a bond between a human and an animal, a bond which has gone beyond mere companionship or friendship and into deeply felt need.

Explication: The second line of the poem states that the lamb's fleece was "white as snow." Similarly, the prophet Isaiah declared, "Though your sins are like scarlet, they shall be as white as snow" (1:18). In addition, Mary has the same name as Jesus' mother. Thus, the lamb thinks of himself as Mary's "savior" and Mary does not disagree: she allows him to tag along wherever she goes.

Reflection: It is as if the lamb needs his surrogate mother (Mary) and Mary needs her Christ child (the lamb).

Speculation: Such behavior is clearly unhealthy and will lead to Mary's dissatisfaction and the lamb will most likely be rejected by his fellow sheep.

Things to note:

- There are numerous comments and *types* of comments that can be made from one quote.
- Comments sometimes take several sentences to express. There are 12 sentences here—stemming from one CD.
- You are trying to link your argument and the text you are dealing with. You want to establish the link and then explore that connection and how it proves your point (how it proves your THESIS—BT or MT).
- The comments should lead the reader into the text and into the explanation or proof that you are trying to give.
- Even if what you are saying is beyond ridiculous (as much of this is), work hard to support and prove your point. You may actually stumble onto new thoughts or ideas that are worth exploring.

Conclusions

As with introductions, there are two types of conclusions: concluding sentences of paragraphs and the concluding paragraph of an essay. These two types of conclusions are defined on p. 6; however, a few words need to be said here.

Conclusion Sentences

These sentences are sometimes called "closure" sentences and are used to end a paragraph. As said earlier, a CL SHOULD NOT JUST REPEAT the BT. It should wrap up your immediate thoughts and begin to lead the reader (i.e., *transition* the reader) into the next paragraph.

Conclusion Paragraphs

A conclusion paragraph is obviously the last paragraph of an essay. As in music, conclusions are essential—the last word or thought the author gets to give. Students find it easy to simply write a sentence or two and then assume they are finished. This couldn't be further from the truth. You see, by the time you reach your conclusion paragraph your thesis should be thoroughly proven or explained. The conclusion is your opportunity to tie all the pieces of your overall argument together. It is your opportunity to explore the ramifications of all that you've developed in your paper. This may only take the form of a sort of summary or a repetition of your key ideas, but your final statement of them and your specific wording can be effective tools in making an impact on your reader.

Conclusions can also be used to introduce a new idea that is related to your topic—one that might warrant further consideration by the reader—but that you don't have time or the need to develop due to the nature of the assignment. Or, you could use your conclusion to make an emotional appeal to the readers, to move them toward your topic in a way you could not do within the body of the essay. The key is conclusions should give your essay a "finished" feeling.

Here's a sample to give you an idea of what we're talking about:

As has been clearly proven, nursery rhymes can be hazardous to the mental and perhaps physical well-being of a child. "Mary Had a Little Lamb," though perhaps "cute" and memorable, is a threat to a child and thus society. Co-dependence can perhaps be dealt with; rebellion can and will be disciplined; but association with the wicked can not and must not be encouraged nor tolerated. Before we know it, children will go from grinning and laughing at the sing-song nursery rhymes to walking around in gangs, defying all authority, and encouraging others to do the same. In a word, the logical end of exposing children to nursery rhymes is anarchy and the end of civilization as we know it.

Works Cited

The Works Cited page can be a jumble of nonsense if done improperly, a fine reference tool if done properly. It is full of names and italicized words and dates and periods and cities…. However, the setup isn't as complicated as it may at first look. You can worry about putting everything in the right order and with the correct punctuation later, but be sure you have the following pieces of information written down when you are gathering sources for your essays:

1. author's name
2. book title (or magazine title or web site name or periodical title)
3. city where book was published
4. name of publisher
5. date the piece was published (if one is given)
6. editor's and/or translator's name (if applicable)
7. page numbers (if you are citing an essay, article, poem, or story)
8. medium of publication (i.e., print, web, interview, etc.)

Below are several examples of how to cite certain types of works. In each set, the first "example" names each part and is punctuated as a real entry should be. The second "example" is an actual source. Pay special attention to punctuation, line spacing and indentation.

If you need more examples or more information on MLA formatting, consult an *MLA Handbook*. A Google search for "MLA citiions" will work. A most helpful website is Purdue Owl. ("Owl" stands for "online writing lab.") This cite is easy to navigate and very informative. http://owl.english.purdue.edu/owl/

ESSAYS, ARTICLES, POEMS, OR STORIES IN A COLLECTION:

Author's last name, author's first name. "Title of essay, article, poem or story." *Title of Collection or Book*. Ed. Editor's first name then last name. Place of Publication: Name of publisher, year published. Page numbers. Medium of publication.

Coleridge, Samuel Taylor. "The Rime of the Ancient Mariner." *The Top 500 Poems.* Ed. William Harmon. New York: Columbia University Press, 1992. 433-456. Print.

- **an introduction, preface, forward, or afterward**

Author's last name, author's first name. Introduction. *Title of book*. By Author's first name then last name. Place of Publication: Publisher, year published. Page numbers. Medium of publication.

Patterson, David. Introduction. *Confession.* By Leo Tolstoy. New York: W. W. Norton & Company, 1983. 5-9. Print.

BOOKS:

- **reference books (encyclopedia, dictionary, etc.)**

For familiar reference books, do not give full publication information:

Author's last name, author's first name [sometimes no author is given]. "Name of article." *Title of Book*. Edition. Year published. Medium of publication.

"Mandarin." *The Encyclopedia Americana.* 1994 ed. Print.

For less familiar reference books, give full publication information. (see http://owl.english.purdue.edu/owl/)

- **Book with one author:**

Author's last name, author's first name. *Title of book*. Place of publication: Publisher, Year of publication. Medium of Publication.

Paton, Alan. *Cry, The Beloved Country*. New York: Scribner, 2003. Print.

- **Book with one author and a translator:**

Author's last name, author's first name. *Title of book*. Trans. Translator's first name then last name. Place of publication: Name of publisher, year published. Medium of publication.

Erasmus, Desiderius. *The Praise of Folly and Other Writings*. Trans. Robert M. Adams. New York: W. W. Norton & Company, 1989. Print.

- **Book with more than one author:**

First author's last name, first author's first name, second author's first name then last name. *Title of book*. Place of publication: Name of publisher, year published. Medium of publication.

Sullivan, Richard E., Dennis Sherman, John B. Harrison. *A Short History of Western Civilization*. 8th edition. Boston: McGraw-Hill, 1994. Print.

➢ Note that the third author is listed like the second author is listed (first name then last name) and that the edition number is placed **after** the title of the book.

FILM OR VIDEO:

Film Title. Dir. Director's name Perf. Names of main actors. Film company, year film released. Medium of publication.

Unforgiven. Dir. Clint Eastwood. Perf. Clint Eastwood, Gene Hackman, Morgan Freeman, and Richard Harris. Warner Bros., 1992. DVD.

ONLINE SOURCES:

- **Personal or professional Web site or page:**

Author's last name, author's first name. "Net page title." *Site title*. Date of publication or latest update. Name of producers of Web page. Medium of publication. Date publication was accessed..

"Frozen Shoulder (Adhesive Capsulitis)." *MCW Healthlink*. 7 May 1999. Medical College of Wisconsin. Web. 7 August 2006.

➢ Note that this particular article has no author listed. Because this is the case, begin with the title of the article.

- **Online book**

Author's last name, author's first name. *Title of book*. Date of original publication. Trans. Translator's first and last name. *Name of website.* Most recent year of website's version of the publication. Medium of publication. Date publication was accessed.

Aurelius, Marcus. *Meditations*. AD 167. George Long. *The Internet Classics Archive*. 2000. Web. 7 August 2006

- **Online article (or abstract) from a printed professional journal:**

Author's last name, author's first name. "Name of article." *Name of online journal* [include volume and issue numbers if available] (Date of publication): page numbers [if available]. Medium of publication. Date publication was accessed.

Shoptaw, John. "Dickinson's Civil War Poetics: From the Enrollment Act to the Lincoln Assassination." *Project Muse* 19.2 (2010): 1-19. Web. 14 March 2011.

Let's face it: making a works cited entry for online information is difficult. However, here are a few key pieces of information to find before you make your citation for an electronic source.

- Author and/or editor names
- Name of the database, or title of project, book or article
- Any version numbers available
- Date of version, revision or posting
- Publisher information
- Date you accessed the material
- URL [Electronic address, printed between carets (<, >)], if required.

Formatting a Paper

There is only one proper format for papers that follow MLA guidelines. However, there are several *ways* to achieve the proper format using a word processing program. The following is a list of instructions for one or two ways of setting up your paper using Microsoft Word (2007 version and newer).

Heading and Title:

Type the heading at the top left of the first page. List your name, your teacher's name, the course name and the date (see box below). On the line immediately after the heading, type your title and then center it. (Highlight your text. Then, under the "Home" tab, there is a tool box called "Paragraph." Click the "Center text" button.)

At this point, your paper should look like this:

Your Name
Teacher's Name
Class Name
Date

Title

Margins:

1. MARGINS are to be 1 inch on the sides, top and bottom. To be sure they are, select the "Page Layout" tab in the tool bar.
2. Select "Margins."
3. Select the option that sets the margins for 1" for Top, Bottom, Left and Right. (If you do not find a pre-set set-up that fits the 1" margin criteria, select "Custom Margins" and set your own.)

Font:

1. You need to use a FONT that is easy to read. The MLA Handbook says use "Times New Roman" or "Courier." However, others are acceptable, like "Garamond" and "Footlight."
2. To set FONT, select the "Home" tab in the tool bar.
3. The font tools will be on the top left side. Select appropriate style and size.
4. Another way to adjust font style, size, and color is to "right click" your text using the mouse.
5. A couple of tool bars will appear. Scroll your cursor over the smaller of the two and select the style, size, color, etc., that you need.

Line Spacing:

1. To adjust LINE SPACING, right click on your text. A tool bar will appear.
2. Select "Paragraph."
3. At "Line spacing" (near the lower right of the box) select "Double."
4. Click on "OK."

Page Numbers:

Page numbers go in the upper right hand corner of each page. Do not try to "guess" where the page number ought to go. That is a pain and you usually won't be able to get the numbers to line up correctly anyway. Though there are other ways to do this, below is one way of inserting page numbers correctly.

1. Select the "Insert" tab on the tool bar.
2. Select "Page Numbers" (near the center of the page).
3. Select "Top of Page."
4. Select "Plain Number 3."
5. After selecting this, your cursor will be flashing in the "Header" box and to the left of your newly inserted page number.
6. Type your last name and press the space bar.
7. Double click below the "Header" box and your cursor will be back in the main part of your text.

At this point, your paper should look like this:

Last Name 1

Your Name

Teacher's Name

Class Name

Date

Title

Sample Papers

The following pages show excerpts from sample papers and works cited pages. The first example is based on the "Mary Had a Little Lamb" essay begun in this booklet. The second serves as an explanation or guide to properly formatting a paper and a works cited page.

Travis 1

M. Kent Travis

Mrs. Russell

History/English 13

August 24, 2011

Nursery Rhyme Nonsense

Fairy tales and nursery rhymes are the stuff of childhood whimsy. Who can forget the happily ever after of Snow White or Sleeping Beauty brought about by a handsome prince and true love's first kiss? Humpty Dumpty and his great wall fall continue to bring the king's horses and the king's men to the rescue. The happy endings and the sing-song delight of nursery rhyme words can shape so much of a child's imagination. However, some of these so-called rhymes can be detrimental to a child's psyche and his moral development. After all, the "rock-a-bye baby" falls out of the tree and the old woman who lived in a shoe whipped (WHIPPED!) her kids soundly and put them to bed! Although these two examples—of many—have surely had their negative effect, the most detrimental of all the nursery rhymes is the beloved “Mary Had a Little Lamb.” “Mary Had a Little Lamb” teaches children co-dependence, out-right rebellion, and to associate with the wicked.

To begin with, “Mary Had a Little Lamb” is detrimental to a child’s psyche because it embraces the concept of co-dependence. The first stanza of the rhyme states that “everywhere that Mary went,/The lamb was sure to go” (*Walt Disney’s Mother Goose* 6). The thought that a lamb would follow a child around is absolutely absurd. However, if a lamb were to follow a child around, as Mary’s did, then it must have been a particularly needy lamb, for it was “*sure* to go” wherever Mary went. A particularly needy creature, human or otherwise, has a tendency toward abnormal behavior. In the case of Mary’s lamb, that abnormal behavior appears to be a form of co-dependence, as if the lamb could not bear the thought of being left alone. Also, as

Travis 6

Works Cited

Dunn, Harry. *Not Now Son! Why Daddy Can't Read Fairy Tales to Little Johnny.* Zippy: Not Too Good Publisher, 2001. Print.

Facea, Bay B. *The Cry of A Child: How Nursery Rhymes Destroyed What Was Otherwise A Happy Life.* Tyler: BooHoo Press, 2003. Print.

The Holy Bible. English Standard Version. Wheaton: Crossway Bibles, 2001. Print.

Walt Disney's Mother Goose. New York: Western Publishing Company, Inc., 1952. Print.

Astudent 1

I. M. Astudent

Mr. Teacherman

History/English 10

July 27, 1996

Sample Paper

Greetings! Here is a sample paper about setting up a paper. Notice how everything above is double-spaced. Also, notice that I have a page number with my last name in the upper right hand corner. On your 8 1/2 x 11 paper, the margins should be **1 inch** all the way around. (The margins here are obviously not to scale. Please pretend that they are. If that doesn't work, try eating some tacos sold by talking animals.) The font size is 12 and no larger and the title is no different from the rest of the text (no fru-fru font, no underline, no italics, etc.). This is the exact format expected at The Brook Hill School for papers and short writing assignments. Follow the instructions on "Formatting a Paper" perfectly, and you will have no problem setting up a paper in proper *MLA Handbook* format.

Astudent 11

Works Cited

The Epic of Gilgamesh. Trans. N. K. Sanders. New York: Penguin Books, 1972. Print.

Homer. *The Odyssey of Homer.* Trans. Richmond Lattimore. New York: Harper Perennial, 1999. Print.

Schlissel, Steve. "Justification and the Gentiles." *The Federal Vision.* Eds. Steve Wilkins and Duane Garner. Monroe: Athanasius Press, 2004. Print.

Sullivan, Richard E., Dennis Sherman, John B. Harrison. *A Short History of Western Civilization*. 8th edition. Boston: McGraw-Hill, 1994. Print.

Virgil. *The Aeneid*. Trans. Robert Fitzgerald. New York: Vintage Books, 1983. Print.

Wiesel, Elie. *Night*. Trans. Stella Rodway. New York: Bantam Books, 1986. Print.

Things to note from the previous page:

- This is a sample Works Cited page, made up of some of the books used at The Brook Hill School or books used for this guide.
- The page numbering follows the numbering of the paper.
- The citations are in alphabetical order according to author's last name (or book title if there is no author or if the author is unknown).
- Citations are *not* indented. If the citation takes two or more lines, the second line and following *is* indented.
- A Works Cited page ONLY includes works actually referenced or quoted (i.e., *cited*) in the essay or paper; therefore, this Works Cited page would only be accurate if the writer actually cited each of the above sources in his essay or paper.
- Hint on formatting the Works Cited page: When typing a Works Cited page,
  - Type all the information like you would a regular sentence.
  - After you have finished, if your citation is more than one line then go to the beginning of the second line and hit "Enter" to separate the two lines.
  - Then hit the "Tab" button to indent the second line.
  - You may have to repeat this process for each separate line of an entry. Remember, the goal is to get your Works Cited to "look right."

Peer & Self-Review

Being able to evaluate your own work, as well as your peers' work, will improve your critical eye and your own writing.Try to get into the habbit of always reviewing and revising your own work before you turn it in.

Many teachers have their own methods and tools to aid in the revision process. When asked to review an essay, use the teacher's perfered method, if he or she has one. Below is a sample Peer and Self-Review/Evaluation form modified from Crider's "Peer-Review Form" found in The Office of Assertion.

Instructions:
Read your peer's or your own essay and comment on the following questions. Try to offer revision advice or notes—either in writing or verbally—to the paper's writer.

1. Does the essay follow the assignment?
2. Is the focus of the essay focused enough, given the assignment's expectations?
3. Is the MAJOR THESIS identifiable, arguable, and clear?
4. Is the introduction strong? Does it offer some sort of outline for the paper and a thesis?
5. Is the body of the essay strong? Does it support and develop the MAJOR THESIS?
6. Is the CONCLUSION strong?
7. Are the paragraphs unified and do they cohere (fit together well)?
8. Is the diction (use of words) appropriate? Precise? Concise? Vivid?
9. Is the grammar and punctuation correct?
10. Is the essay formatted properly?

Index:

NOTES:

Made in the USA
Columbia, SC
14 August 2019